Aa

apple

A is for Apple

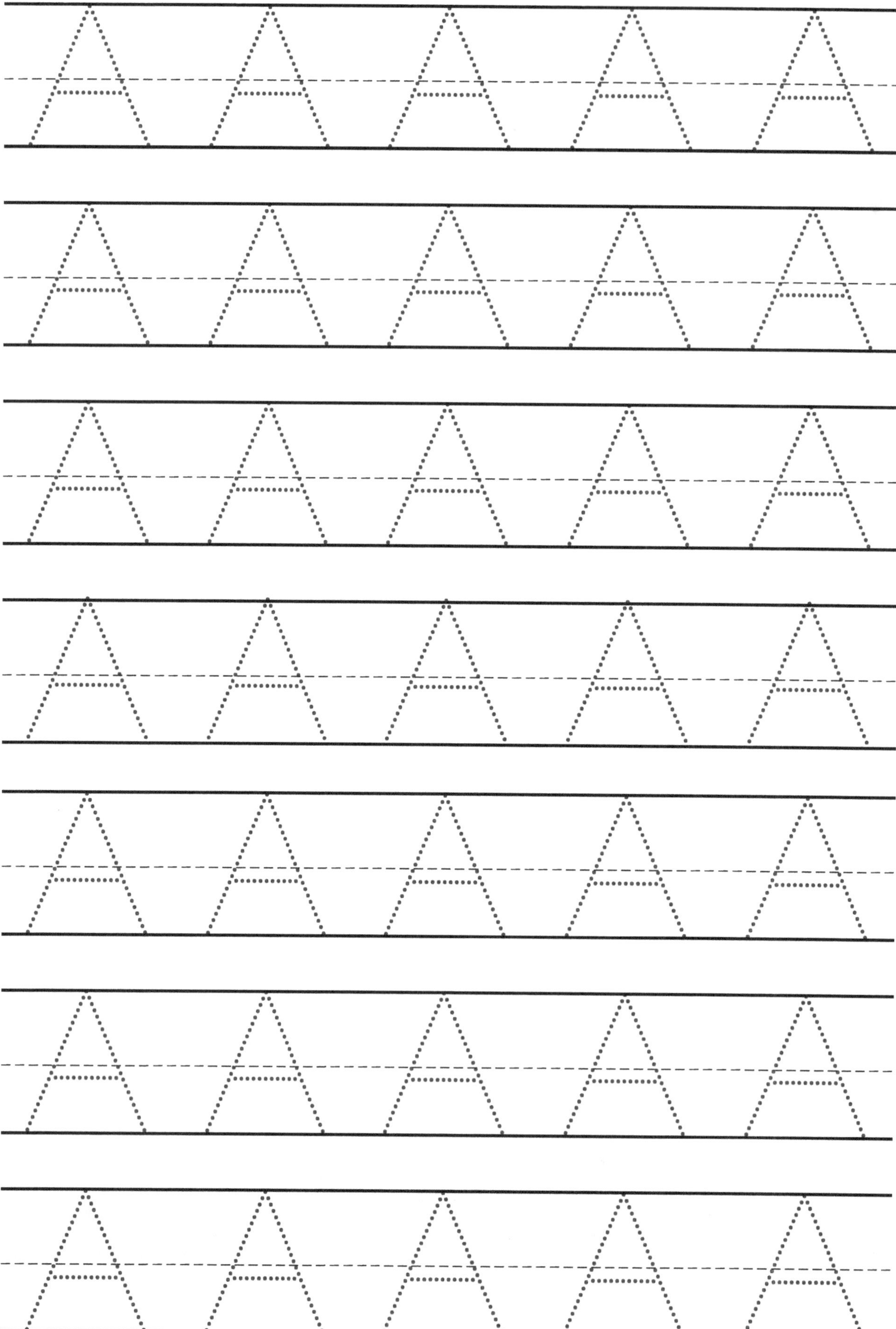

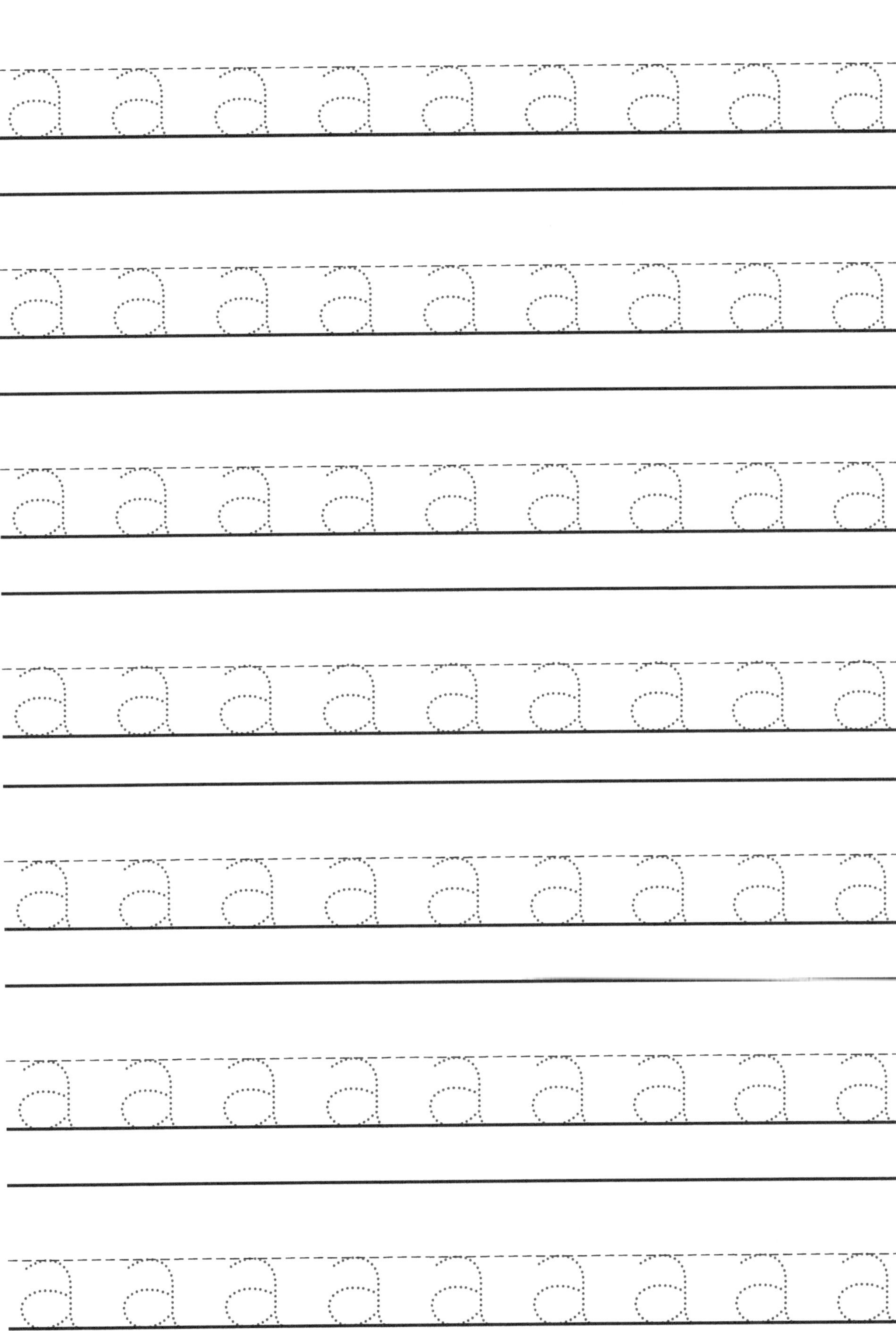

Bb

banana

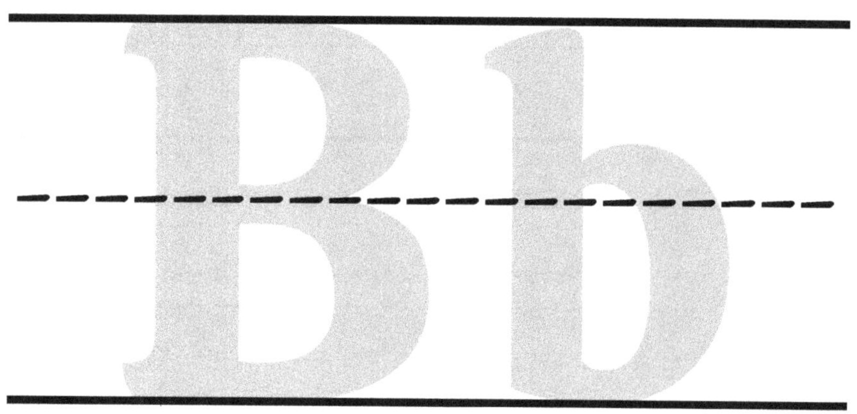

B is for Banana

b b b b b

b b b b b

b b b b b

b b b b b

b b b b b

b b b b b

b b b b b

Cc

cat

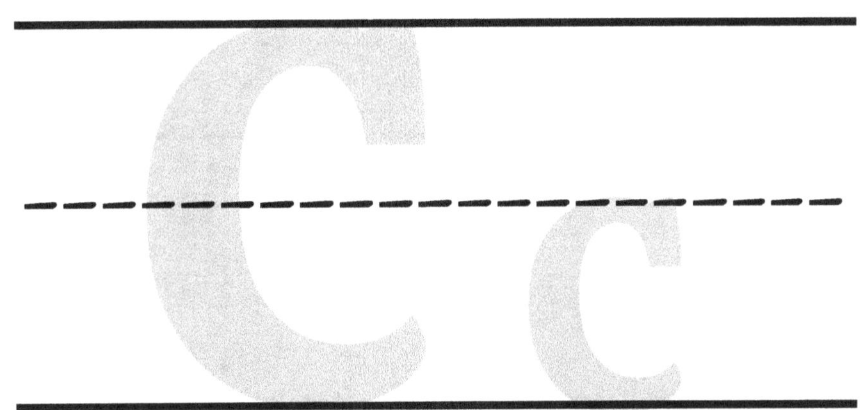

C is for Cat

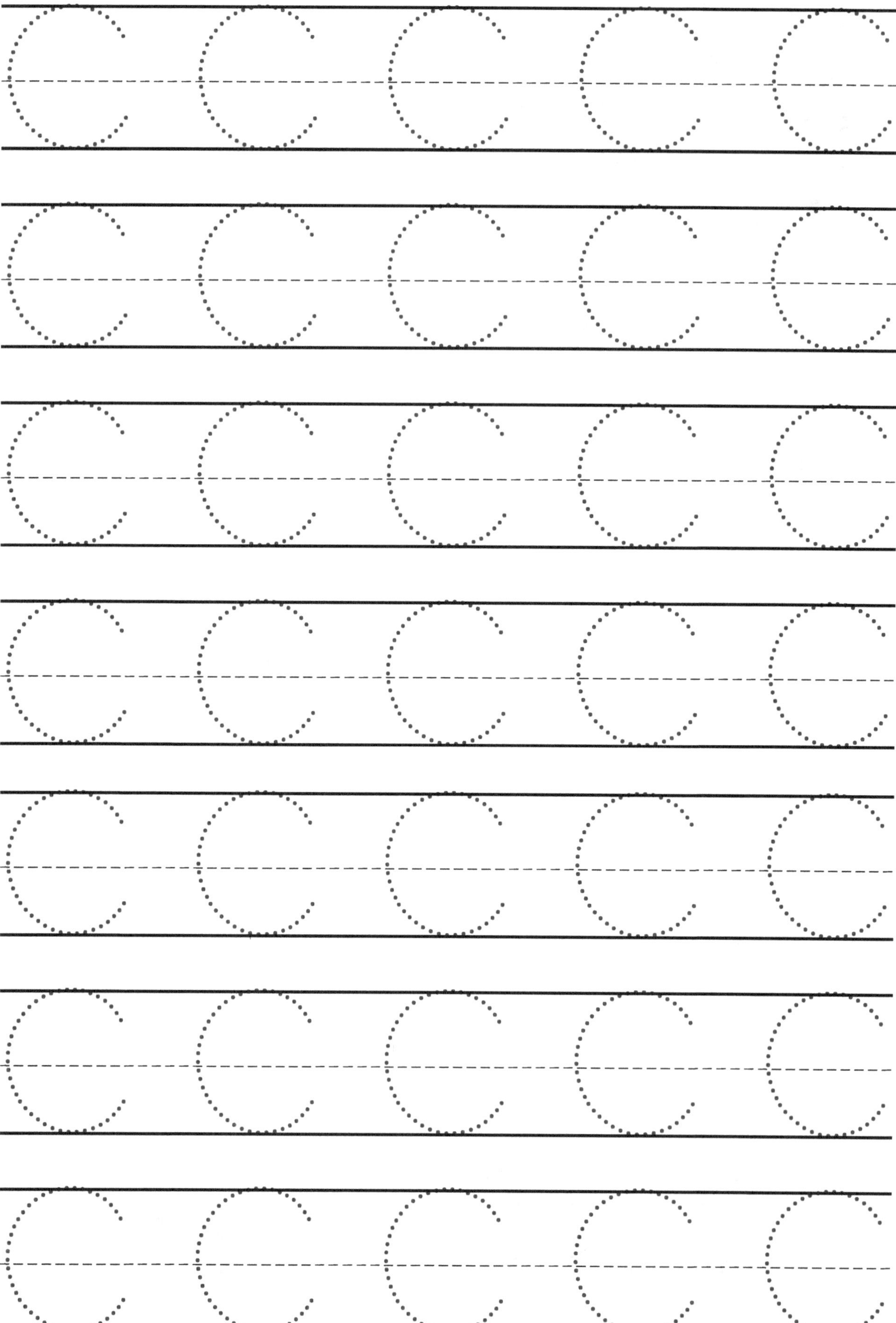

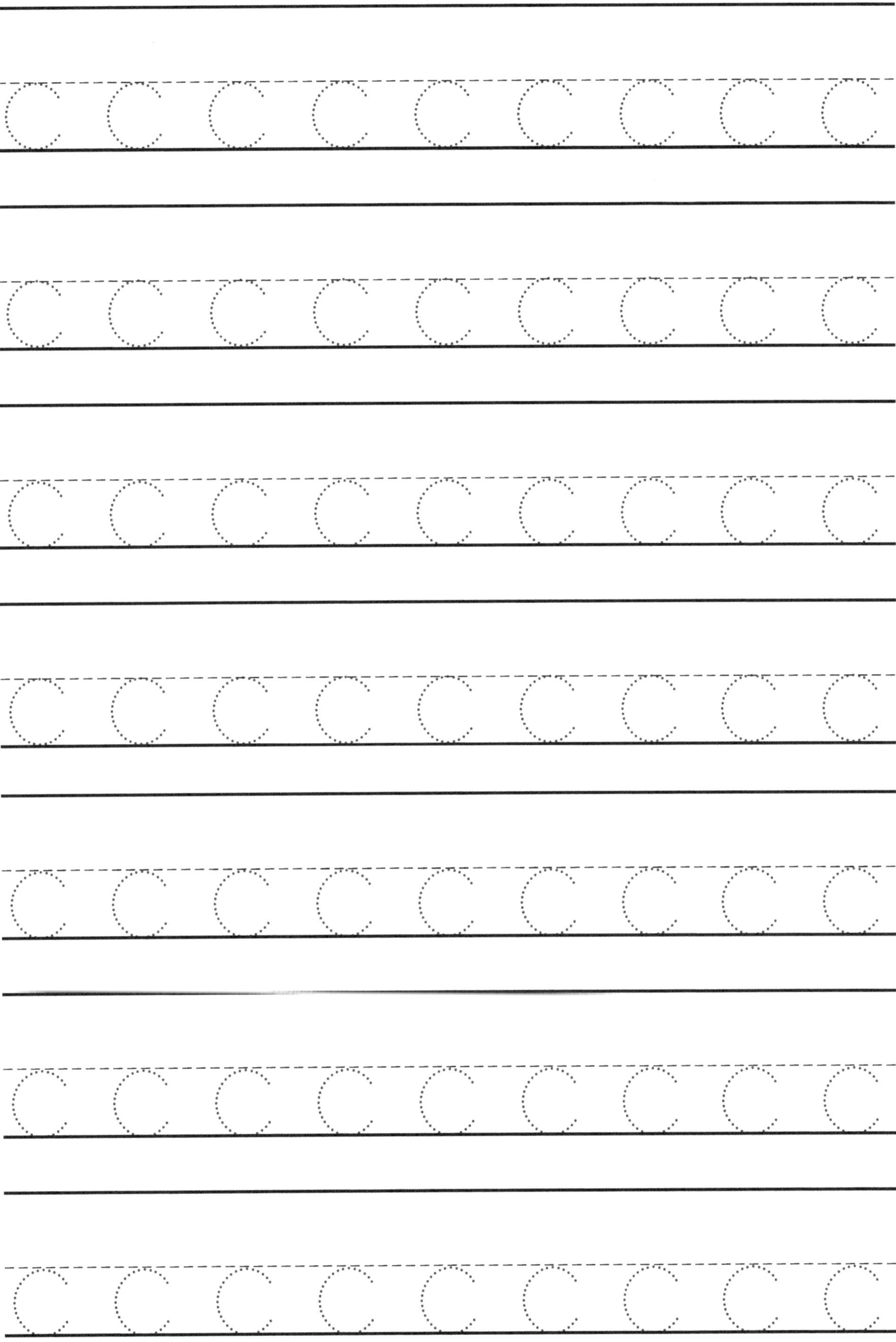

Dd

dinosaur

D is for Dinosaur

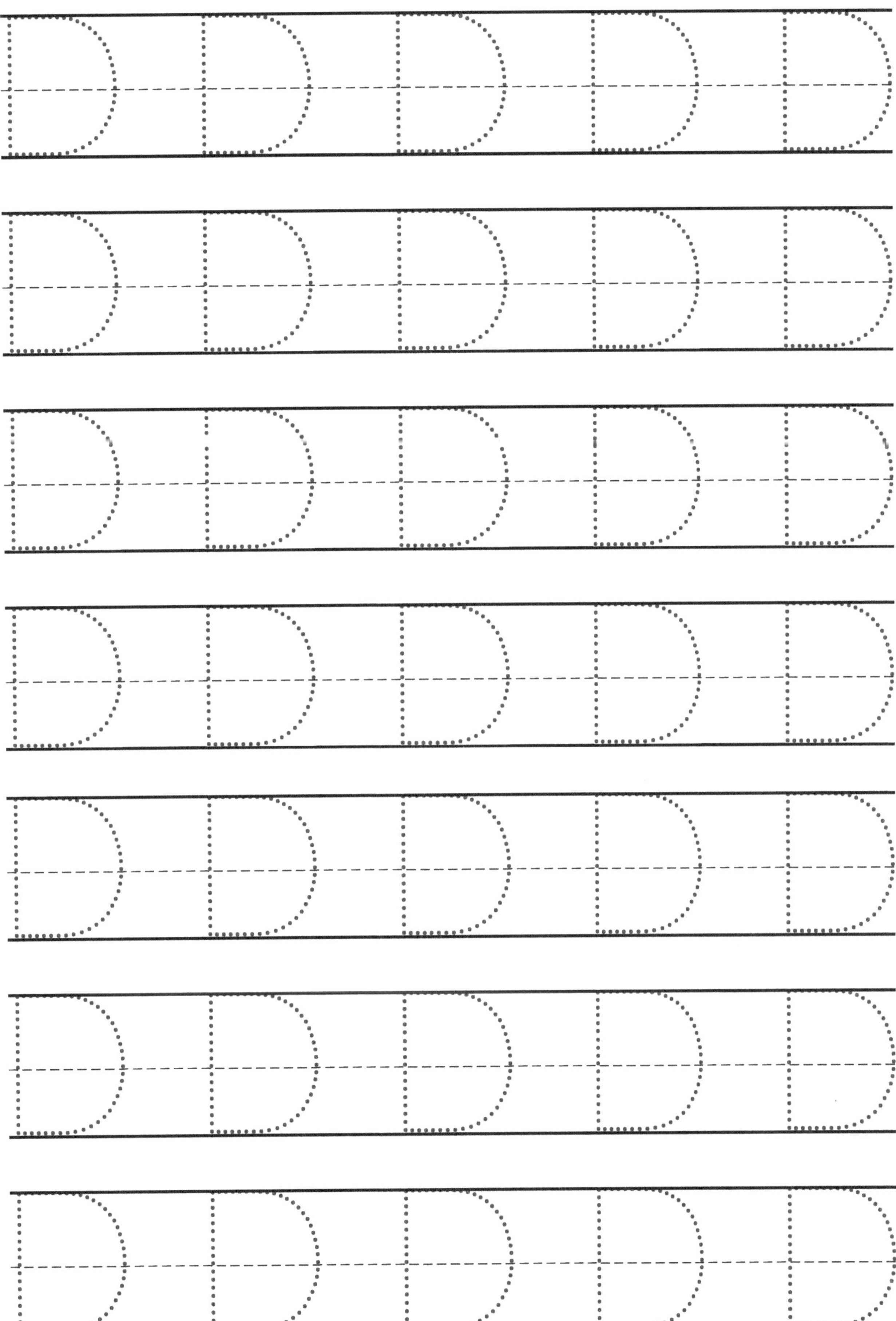

d d d d d d d d

d d d d d d d d

d d d d d d d d

d d d d d d d d

d d d d d d d d

d d d d d d d d

d d d d d d d d

Ee

elephant

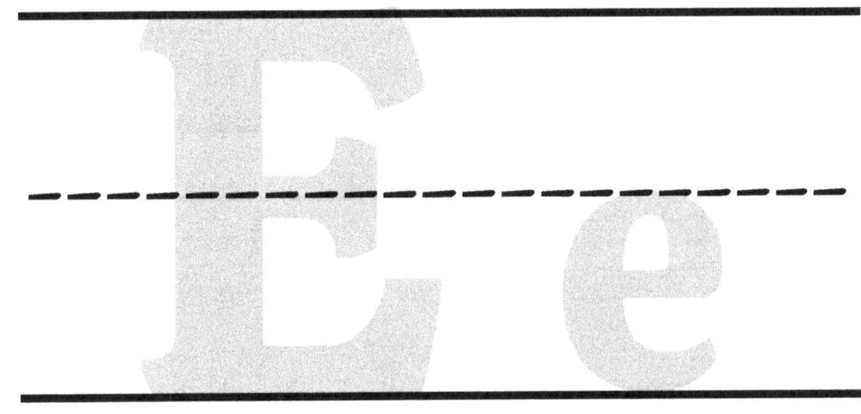

E is for Elephant

Ff

fish

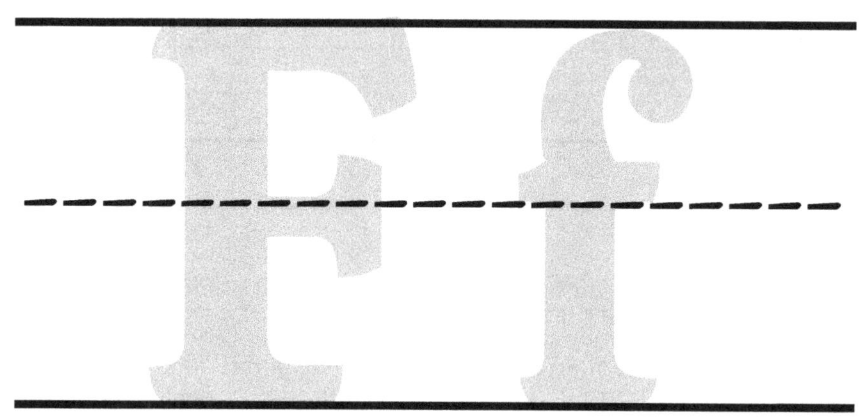

F is for Fish

Gg

giraffe

G is for Giraffe

G G G G G

G G G G G

G G G G G

G G G G G

G G G G G

G G G G G

G G G G G

Hh

house

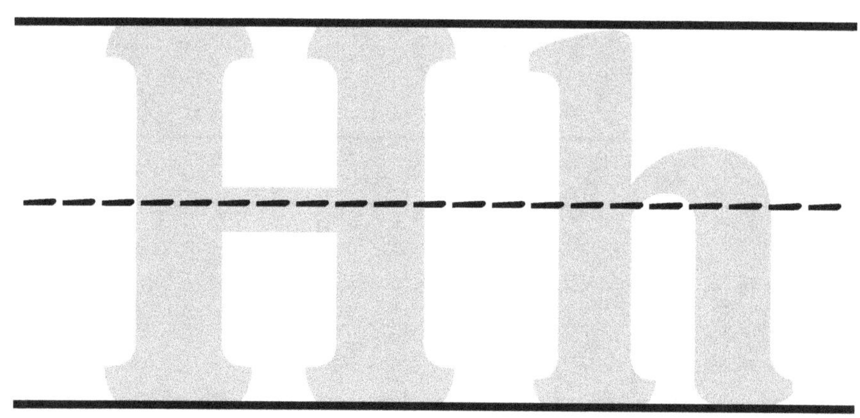

H is for House

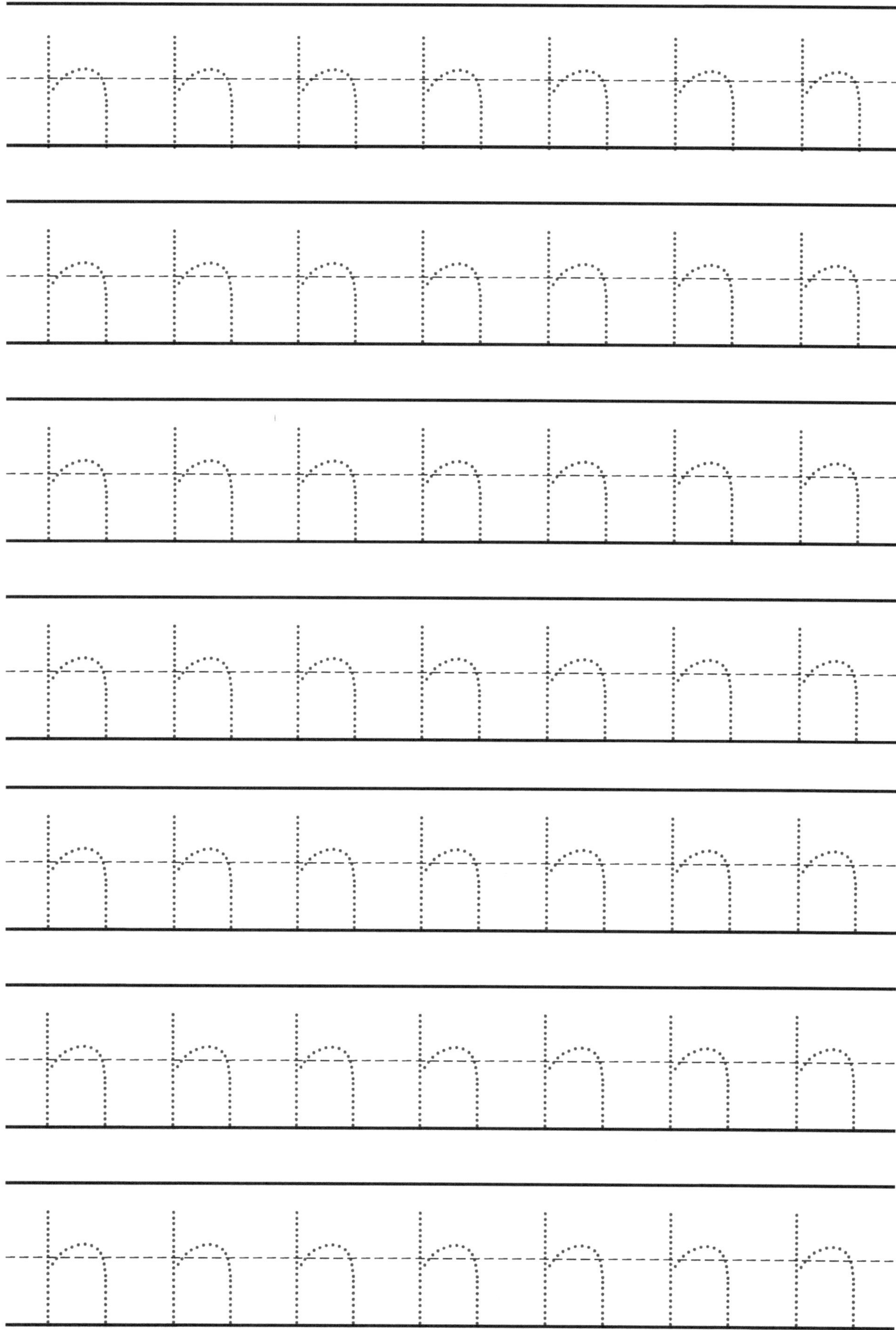

Ii

Ice Cream

I is for Ice Cream

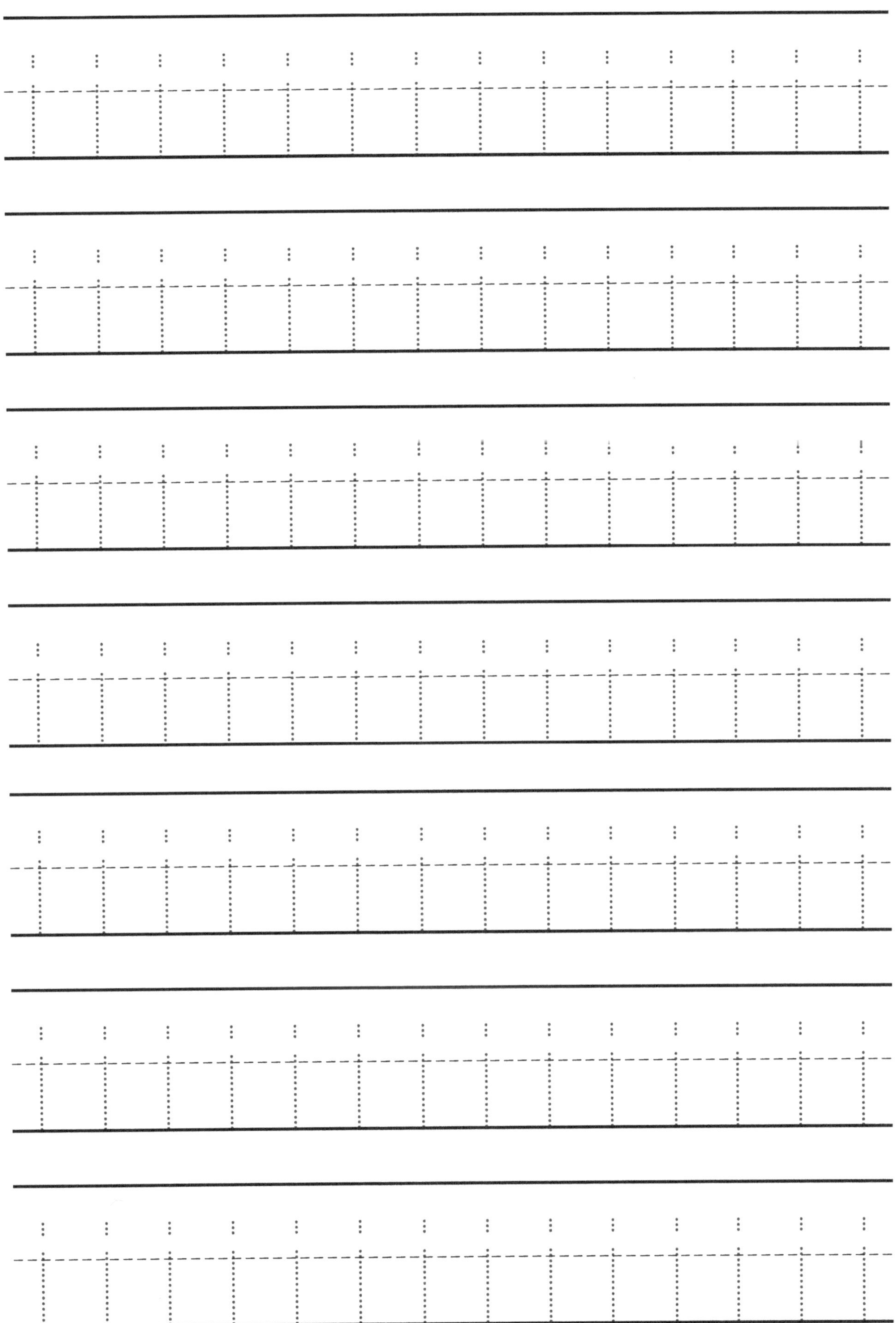

Jj

Juice

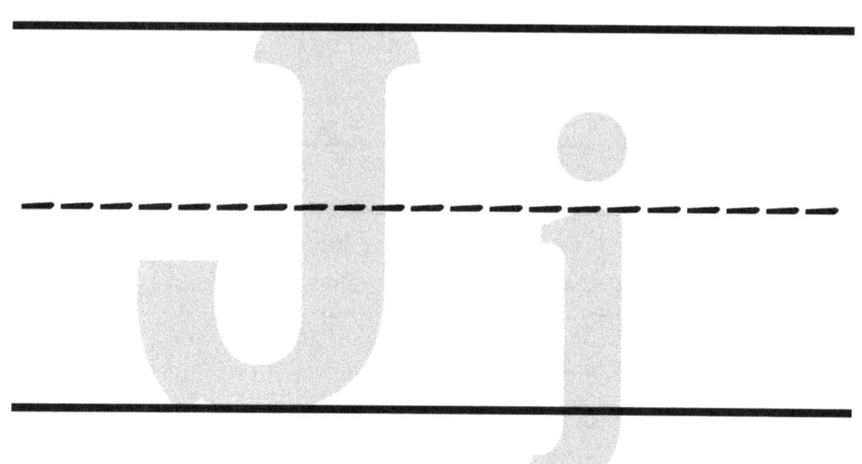

J is for Juice

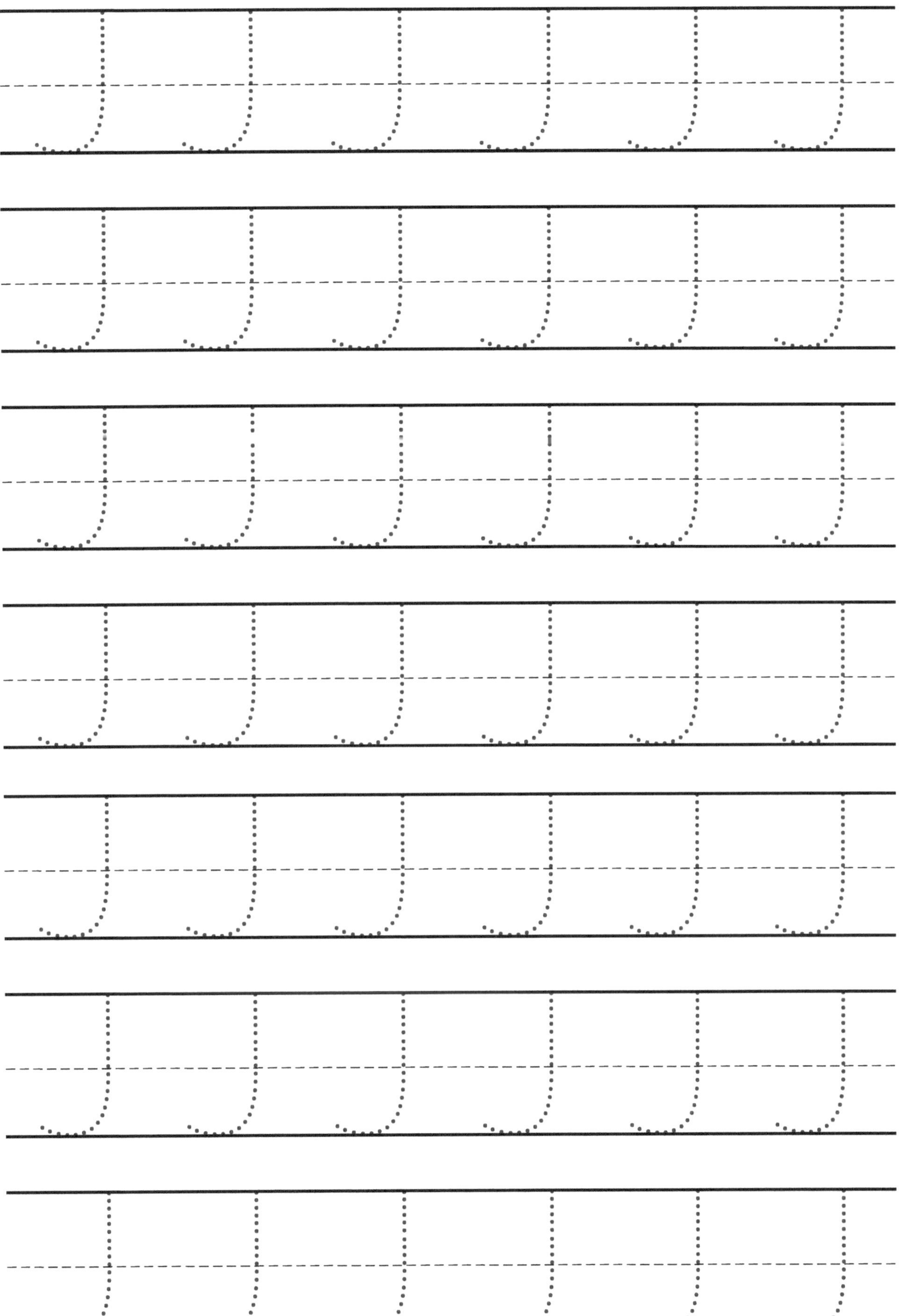

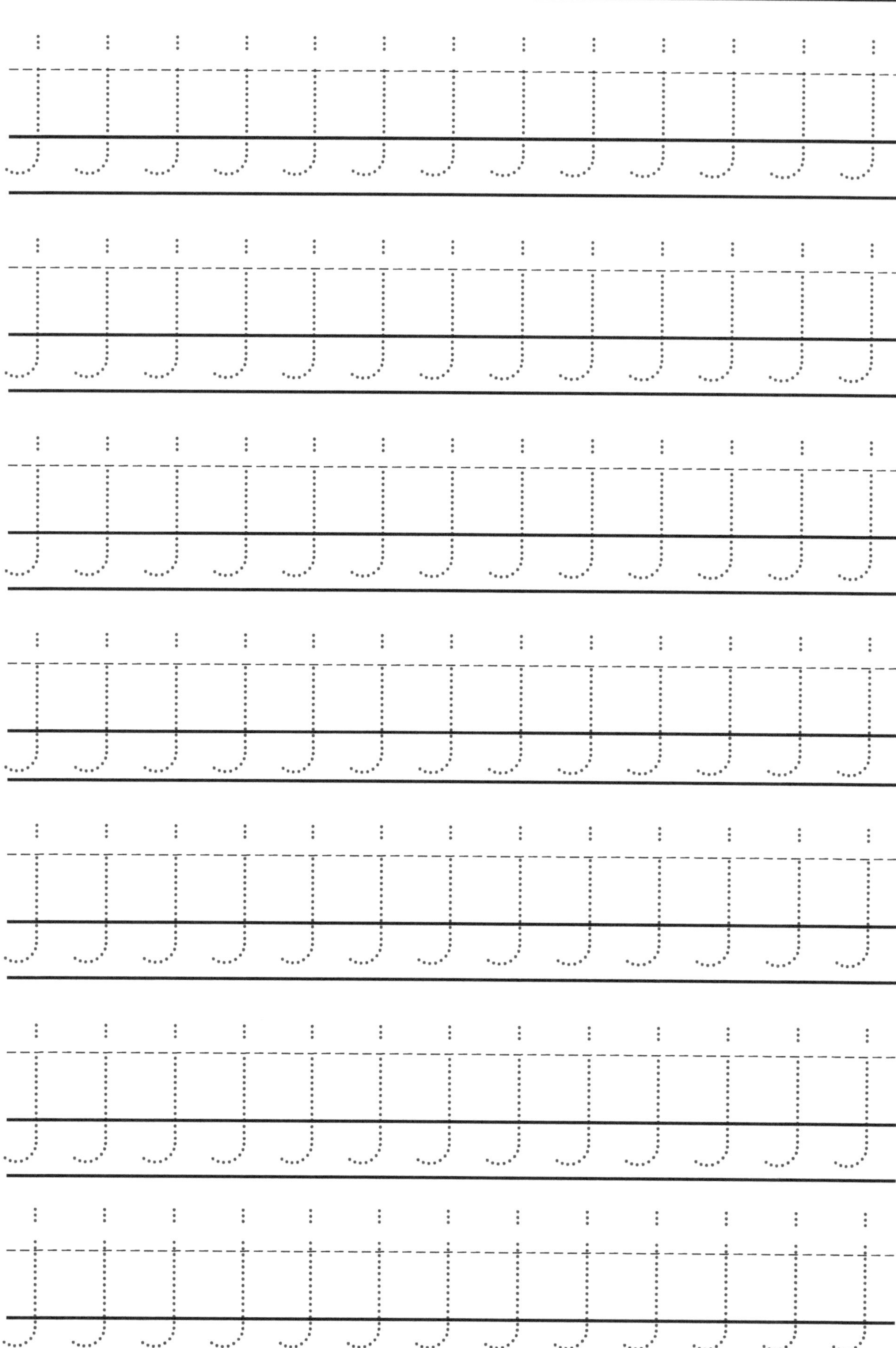

K k

Kite

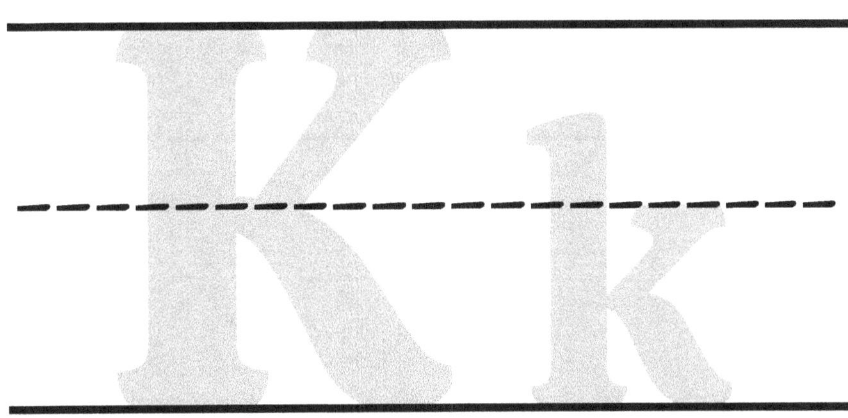

K is for Kite

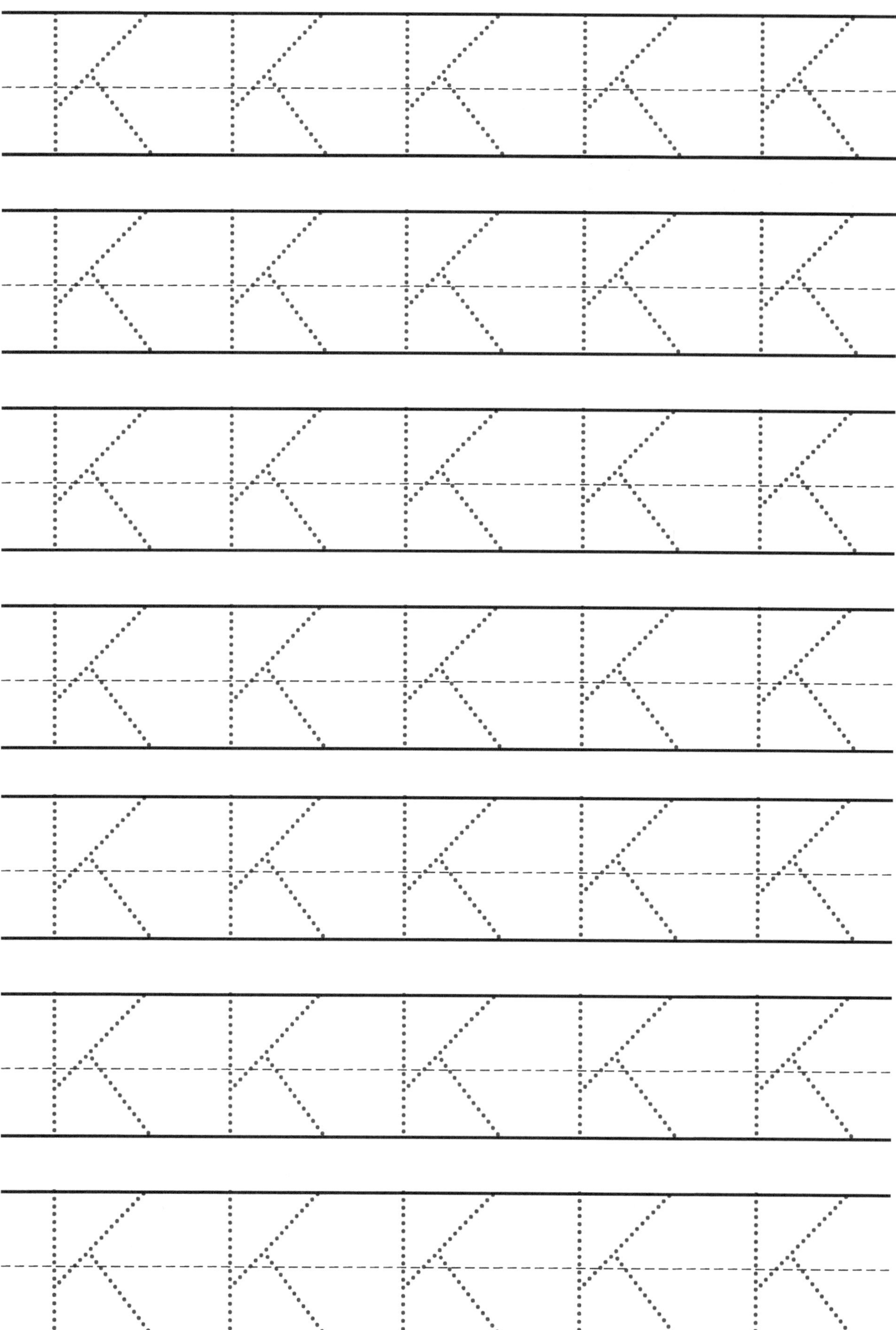

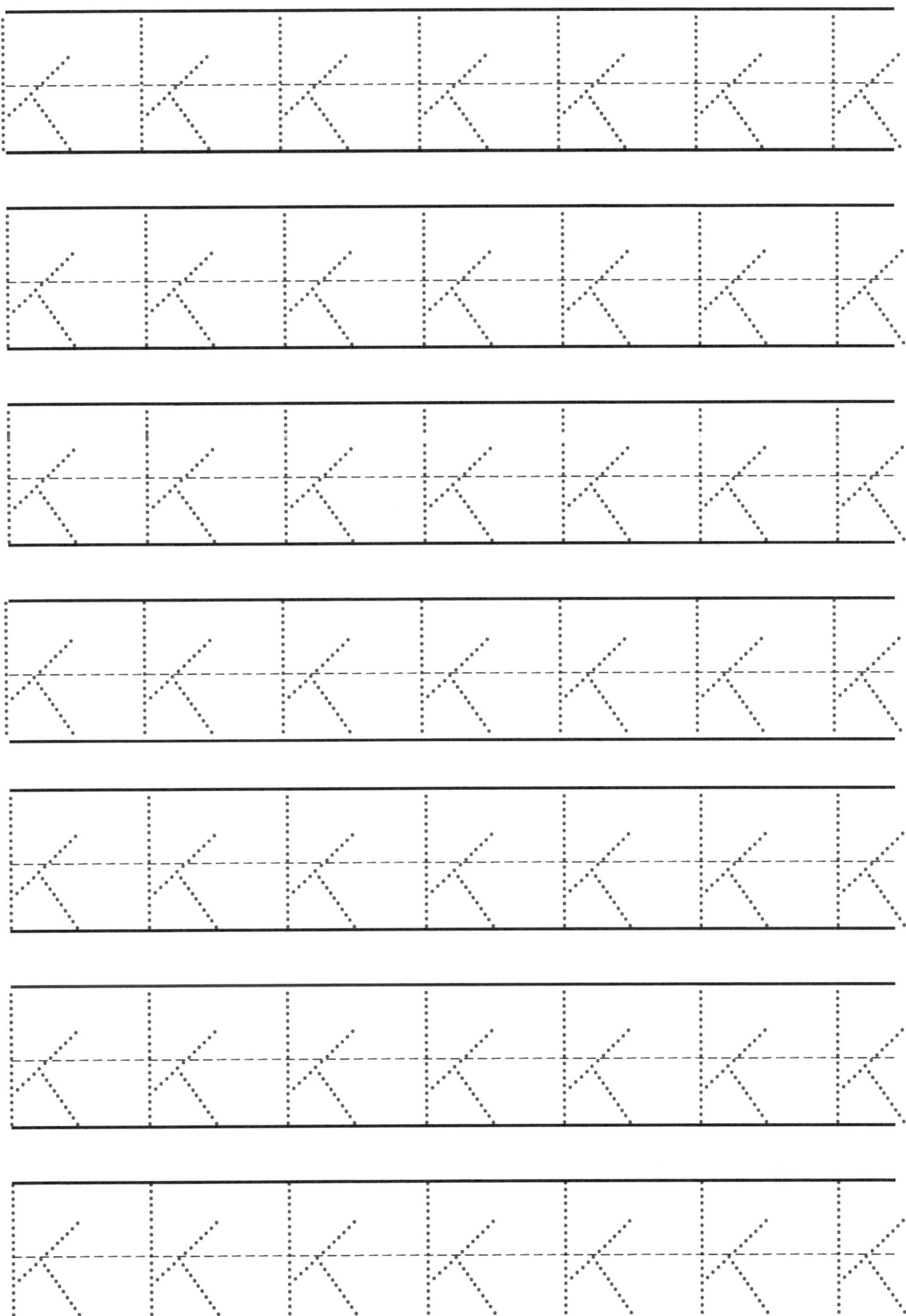

L l

Ladybug

L is for Ladybug

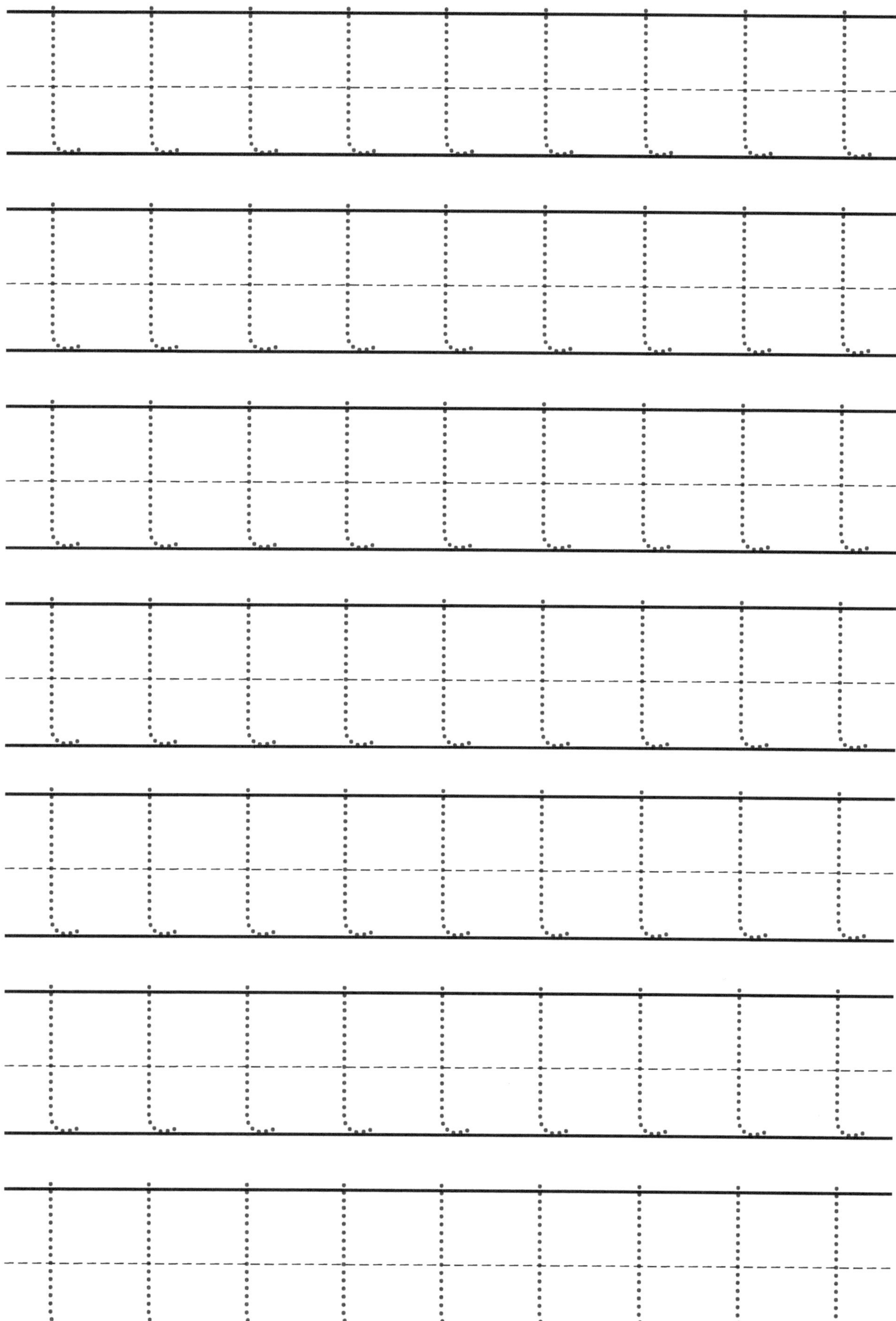

Mm

Monkey

M is for Monkey

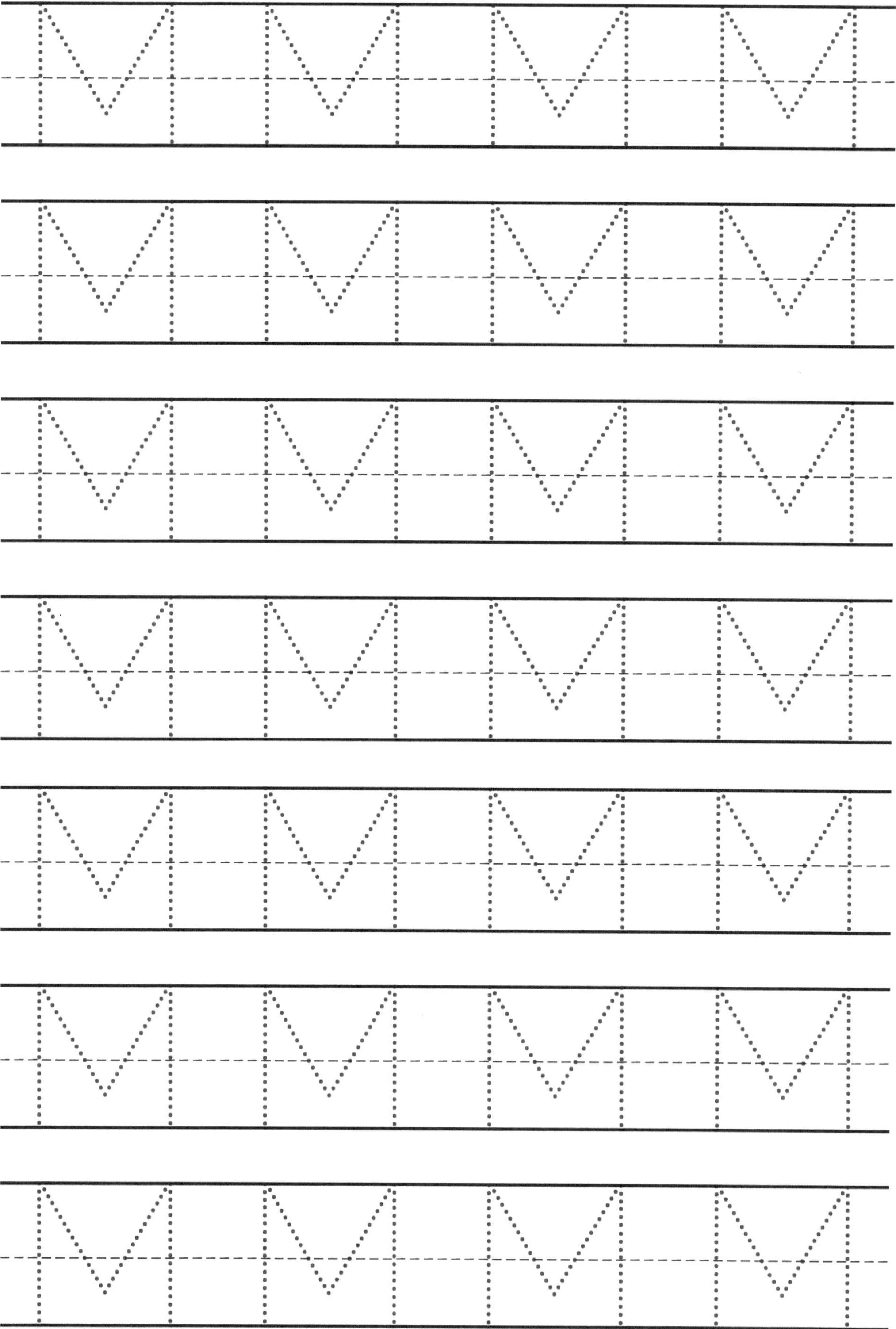

Nn

Nest

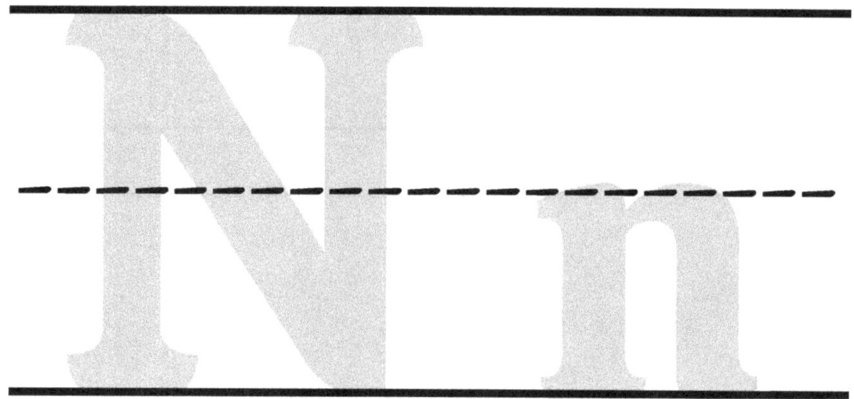

N is for Nest

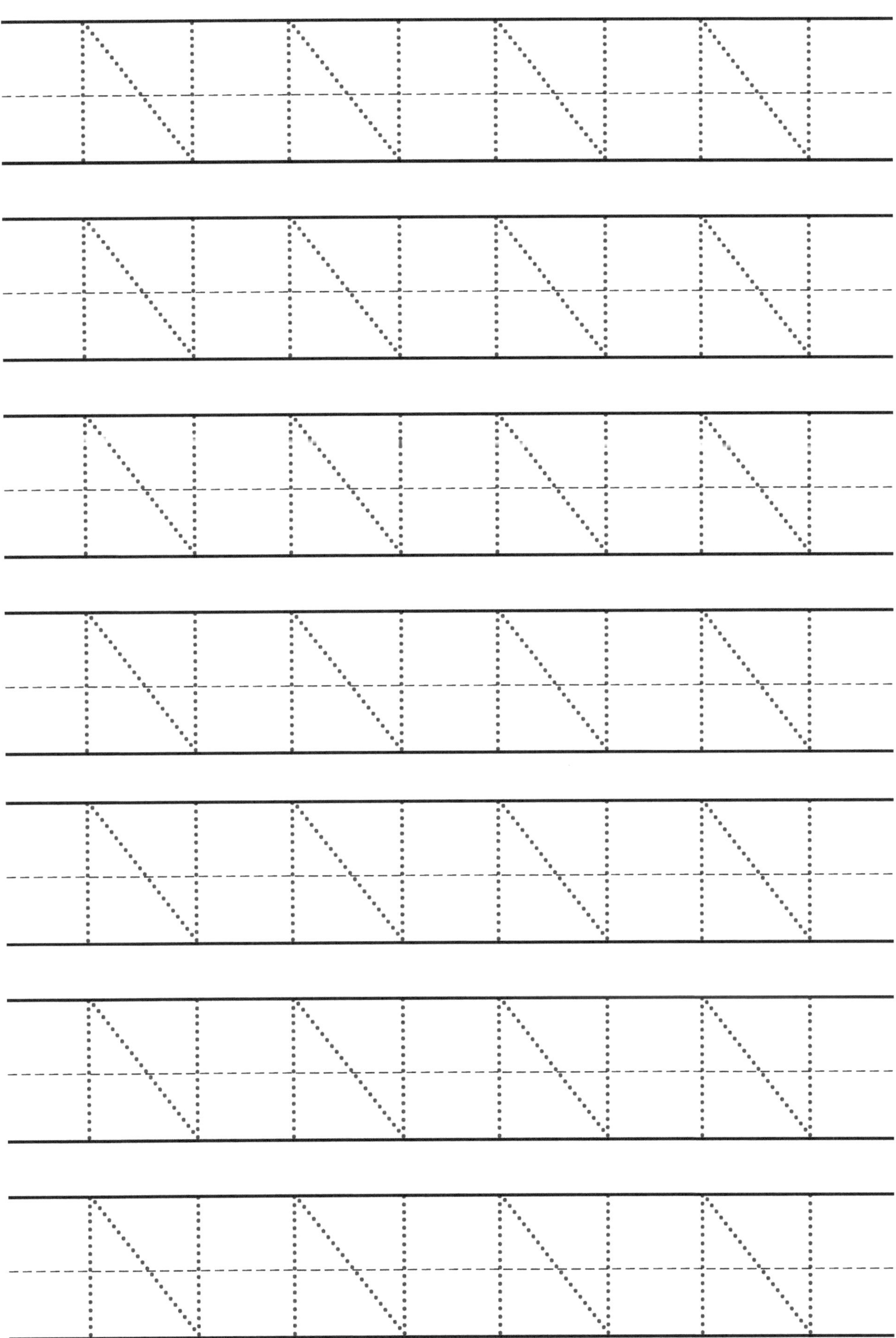

Oo

Orange

O is for Orange

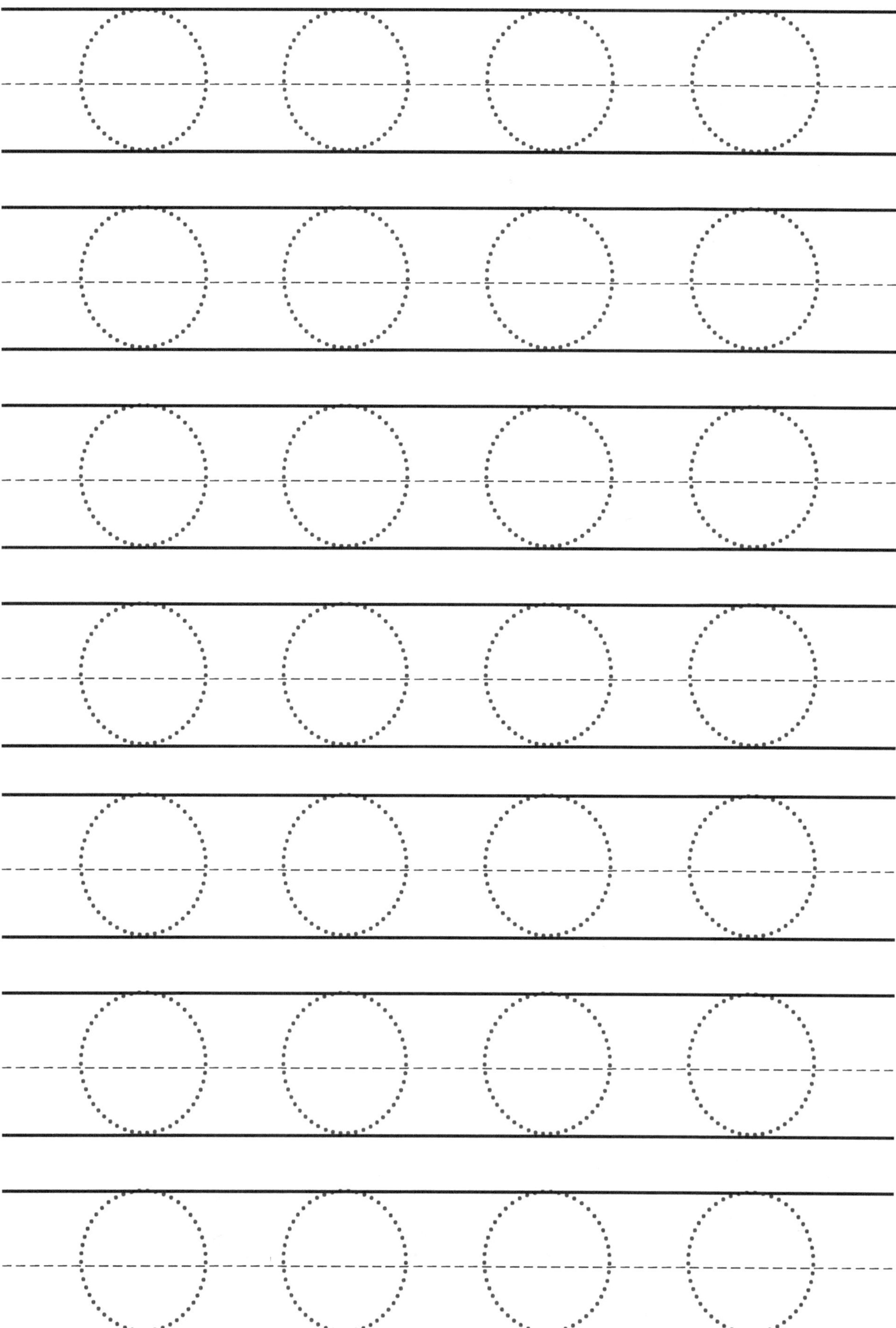

Pp

Penguin

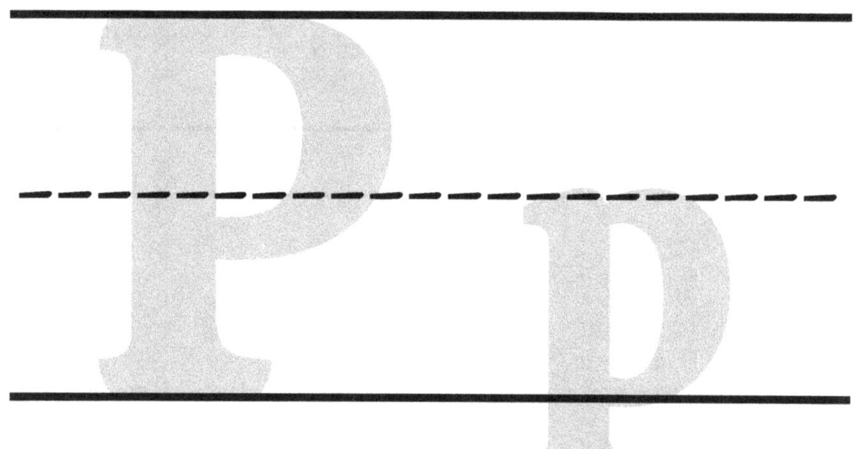

P is for Penguin

P P P P P

P P P P P

P P P P P

P P P P P

P P P P P

P P P P P

P P P P P

p p p p p p p p

p p p p p p p p

p p p p p p p p

p p p p p p p p

p p p p p p p p

p p p p p p p p

p p p p p p p p

Qq

Question

Q is for Question

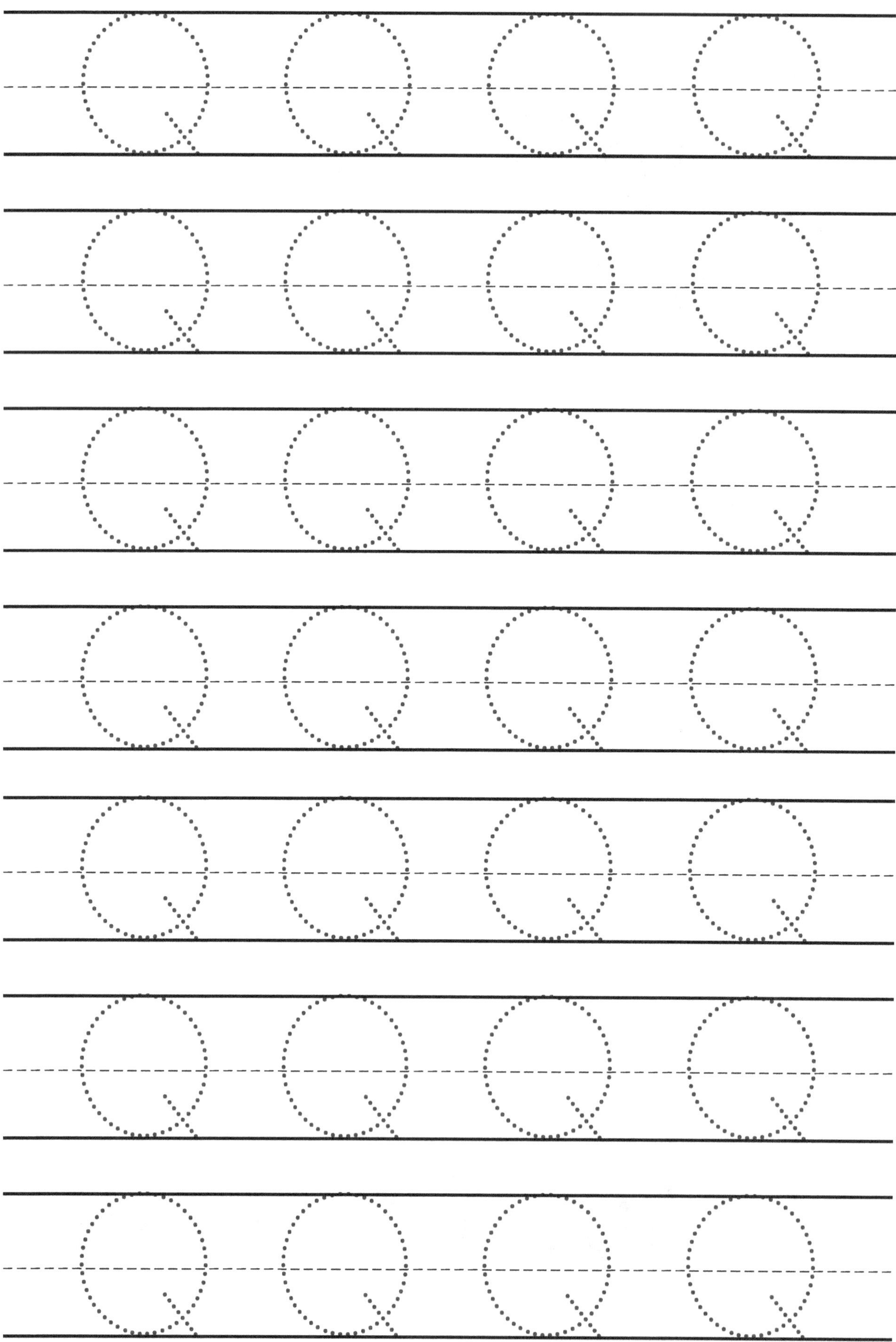

a a a a a a a

a a a a a a a

a a a a a a a

a a a a a a a

a a a a a a a

a a a a a a a

a a a a a a a

Rr

Rocket

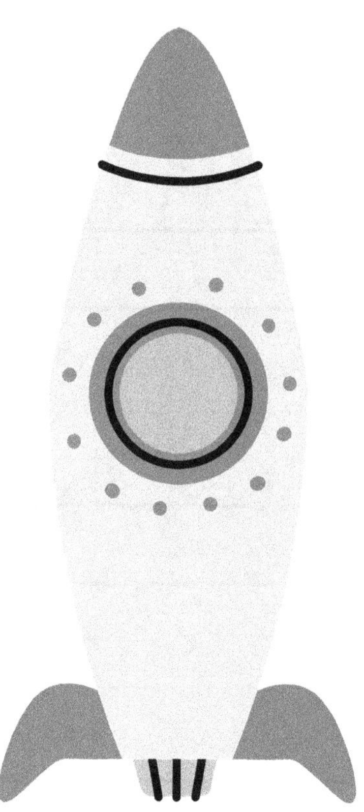

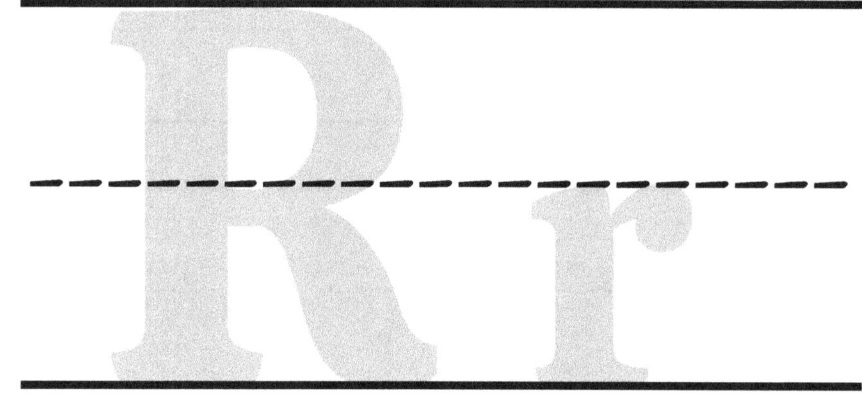

R is for Rocket

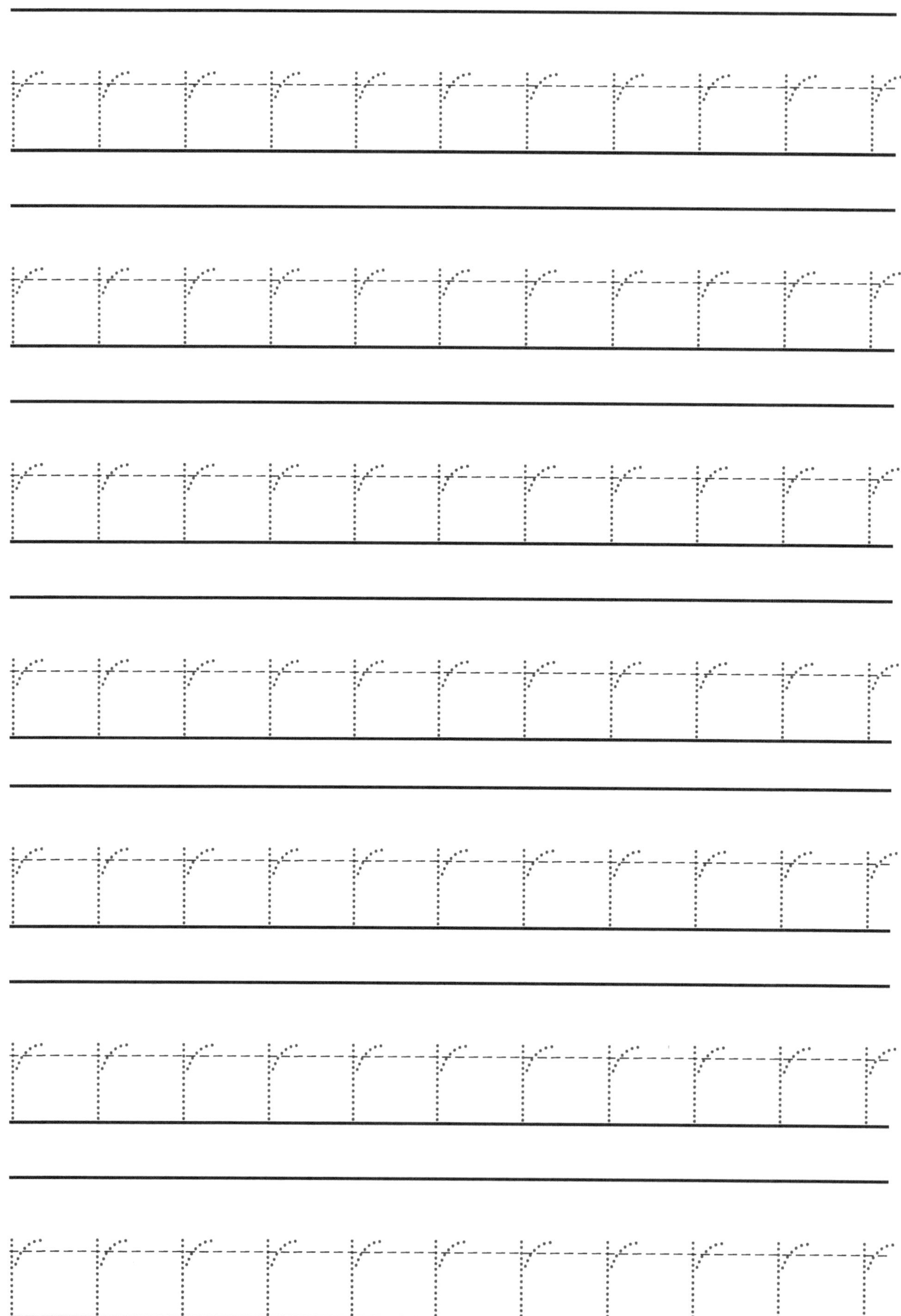

Ss

Sun

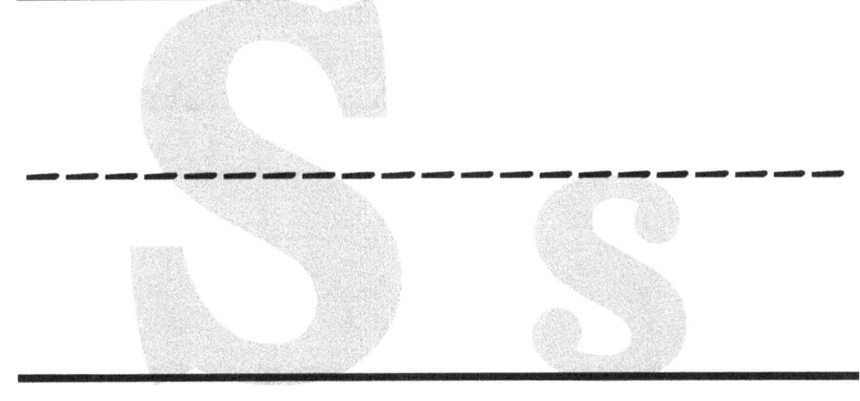

S is for Sun

S S S S S

S S S S S

S S S S S

S S S S S

S S S S S

S S S S S

S S S S S

Tt

Tree

T is for Tree

Uu

Umbrella

U is for Umbrella

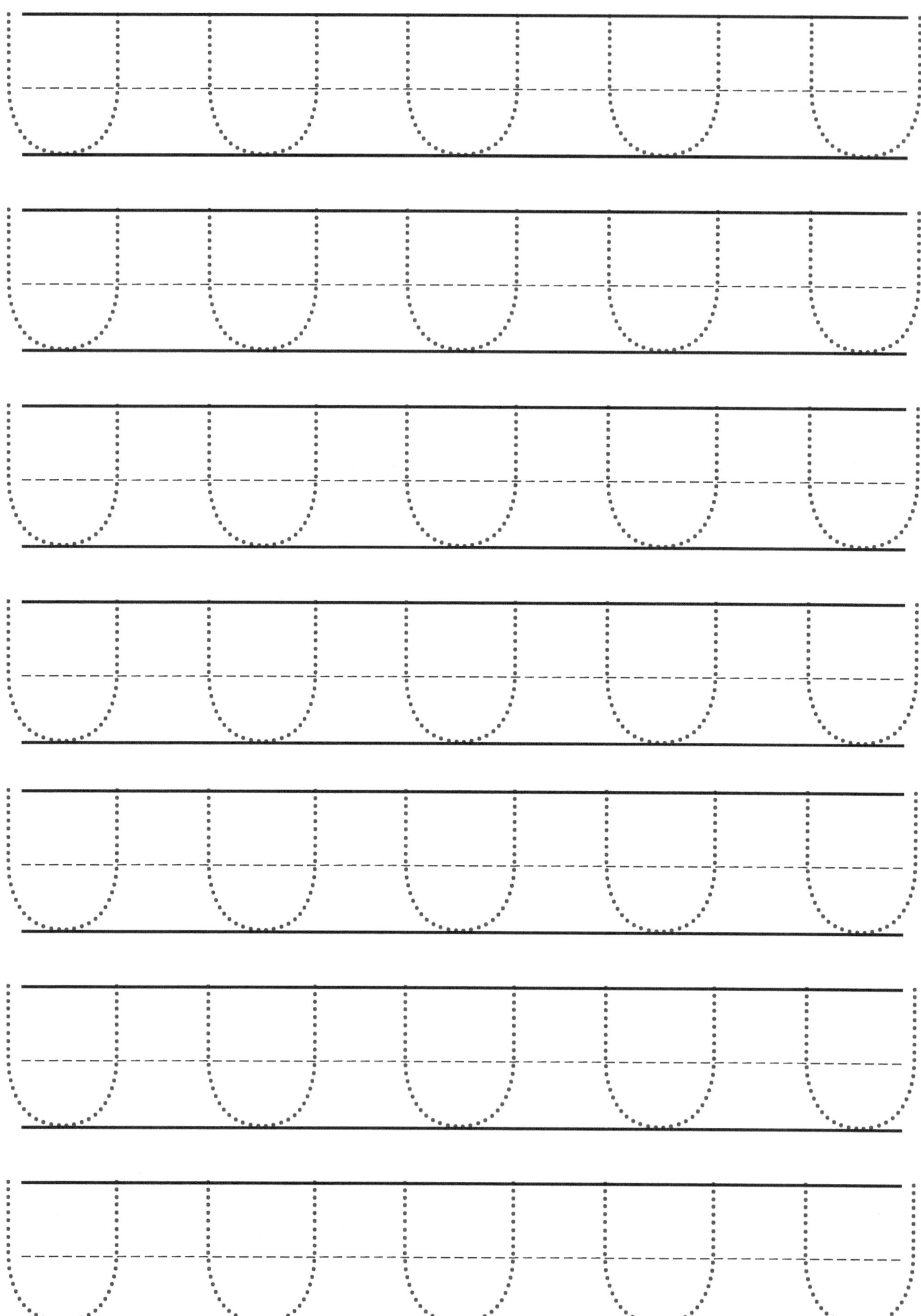

Vv

Volcano

V is for Volcano

Ww

Watch

W is for Watch

Xx

Xylophone

X is for Xylophone

Yy

Yacht

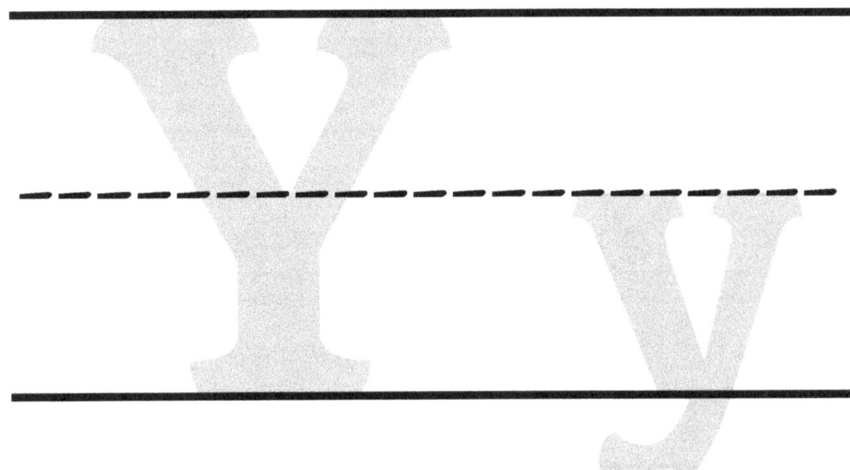

Y is for Yacht

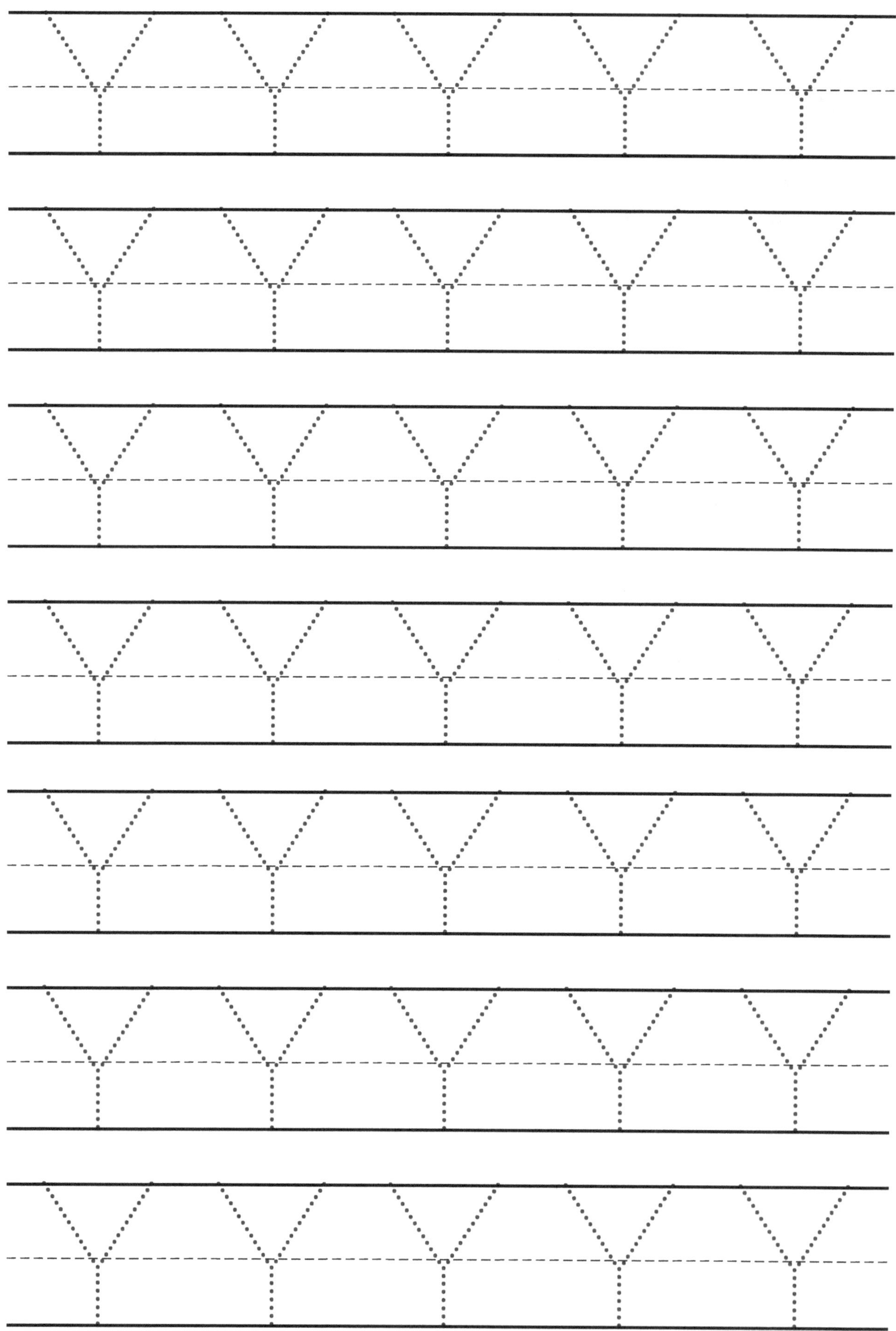

Z z

Zebra

Z is for Zebra

CURSIVE HANDWRITING
Numbers Workbook

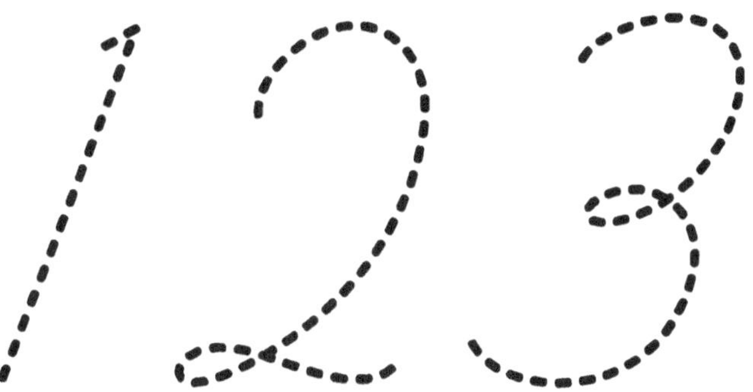

This book belongs to:

0
ZERO
Zero

1

One

2

Two

3

Three

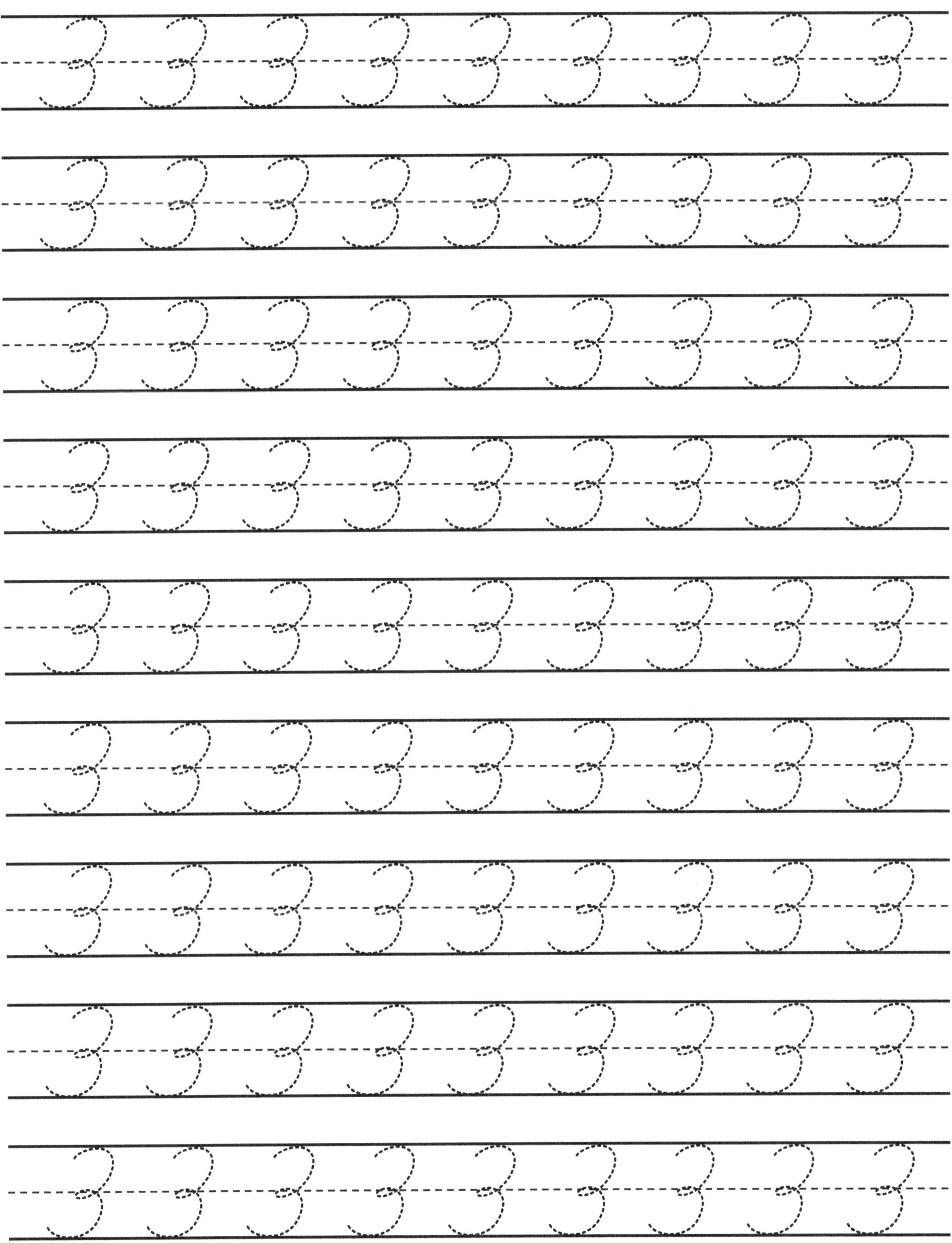

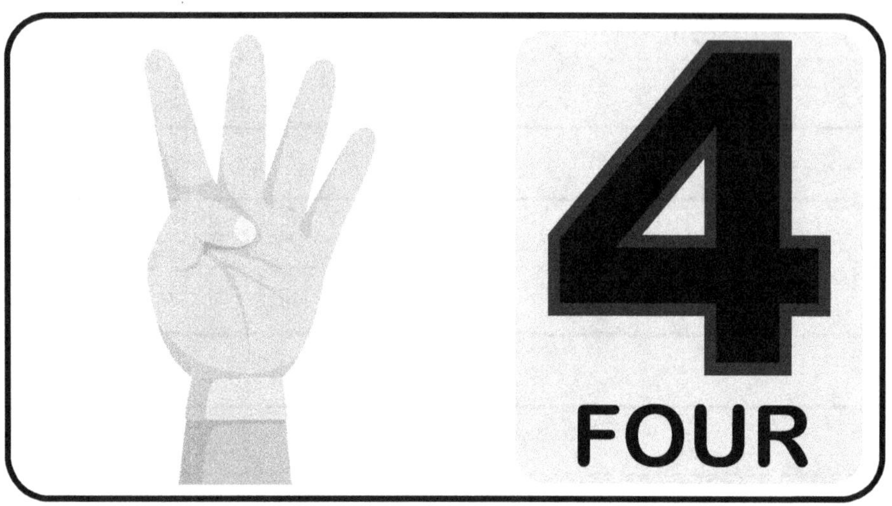

4

4 4 4 4 4 4 4 4 4

4 4 4 4 4 4 4 4 4

4 4 4 4 4 4 4 4 4

Four

Four Four Four

Four Four Four

Four Four Four Four

5

5 5 5 5 5 5 5 5

5 5 5 5 5 5 5 5

5 5 5 5 5 5 5 5

Five

Five Five Five

Five Five Five

Five Five Five Five

5 5 5 5 5 5 5 5 5

5 5 5 5 5 5 5 5 5

5 5 5 5 5 5 5 5 5

5 5 5 5 5 5 5 5 5

5 5 5 5 5 5 5 5 5

5 5 5 5 5 5 5 5 5

5 5 5 5 5 5 5 5 5

5 5 5 5 5 5 5 5 5

5 5 5 5 5 5 5 5 5

6

6 6 6 6 6 6 6

6 6 6 6 6 6 6 6 6 6

Six

Six Six Six

Six Six Six Six Six

7

Seven

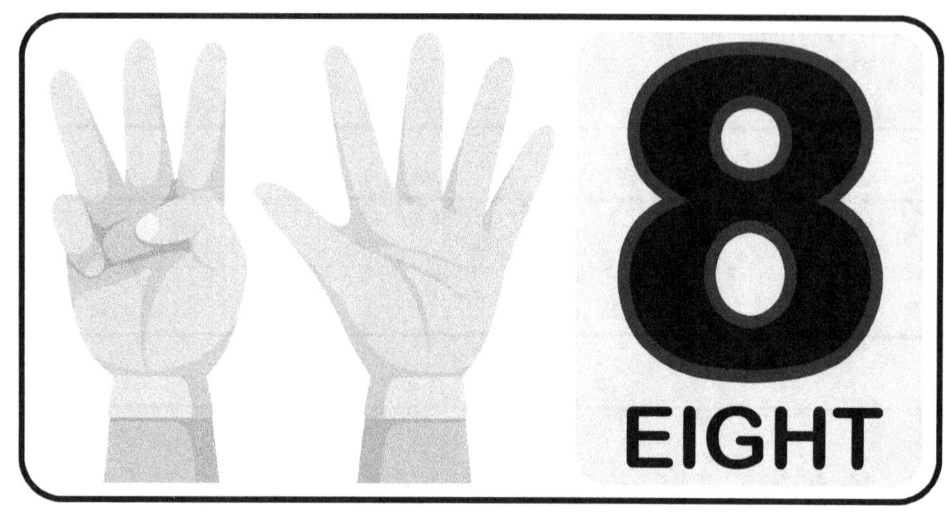

8

8 8 8 8 8 8 8

8 8 8 8 8 8 8 8 8 8

Eight

Eight   Eight

Eight   Eight   Eight

9

Nine

9 9 9 9 9 9 9 9 9 9 9

9 9 9 9 9 9 9 9 9 9 9

9 9 9 9 9 9 9 9 9 9 9

9 9 9 9 9 9 9 9 9 9 9

9 9 9 9 9 9 9 9 9 9 9

9 9 9 9 9 9 9 9 9 9 9

9 9 9 9 9 9 9 9 9 9 9

9 9 9 9 9 9 9 9 9 9 9

9 9 9 9 9 9 9 9 9 9 9

10

10 10 10 10 10

10 10 10 10 10

10 10 10 10 10 10 10

Ten

Ten Ten Ten Ten

Ten Ten Ten Ten

Ten Ten Ten Ten Ten